For the stray in each of us. And for little Bird Lipton.

A FEIWEL AND FRIENDS BOOK
An Imprint of Macmillan Publishing Group, LLC
120 Broadway, New York, NY 10271
mackids.com

Our books may be purchased in bulk for promotional, educational, or business use.
Please contact your local bookseller or the Macmillan Corporate and Premium Sales
Department at (800) 221-7945 ext. 5442 or by email at MacmillanSpecialMarkets@macmillan.com.

Library of Congress Control Number: 2022949544

First edition, 2023
Book design by Mina Chung
The artist used acrylic gouache on Bristol board to create the illustrations for this book.
Feiwel and Friends logo designed by Filomena Tuosto
Printed in China by RR Donnelley Asia Printing Solutions Ltd., Dongguan City, Guangdong Province

ISBN 978-1-250-86476-5 (hardcover)
1 3 5 7 9 10 8 6 4 2

How Mr. Silver Stole the Show

Written by
Kate Klise

Illustrated by
M. Sarah Klise

Feiwel and Friends • New York

Think back to a long-ago Thursday morning in 1947.
A cold November rain was lashing the roofs and streets
of St. Louis, Missouri.

Inside the Hamilton Hotel, guests lingered over their breakfasts while in the kitchen, the staff was busy ironing napkins and polishing silverware.

"What lousy weather," said the headwaiter.

"You've got that right," said a young busboy.

"Supposed to rain all day," added the chef.
No one noticed the piece of bread burning in the toaster.

No one, that is, except Miss Marcella Duffy. She was the hostess of the Hamilton Hotel, one of the city's finest hotels. It was built to accommodate travelers arriving for the 1904 World's Fair. Since then, the Hamilton Hotel had welcomed guests from all over the world who came to the hotel expecting first-class service—not the smell of burned toast.

"I had a hunch this newfangled toaster would be a problem," Miss Duffy said as she carried the charred toast across the kitchen.

She used her hip to open the back door.

That's when Marcella Duffy saw him: a dark gray kitten, shivering in
the alley behind the hotel.

"Oh, you poor dear," said Miss Marcella Duffy. "It's too miserable to
be outside today. Go home."

But the kitten didn't move. He just stared blankly at the hostess.

"No collar, huh?" Marcella Duffy said. "What's your name? Where's your family?"

The kitten didn't mew or purr. He shifted his gaze to the piece of toast.

"You must be starving," Miss Duffy said. "We can do better than burned toast." She turned to speak to her colleagues in the kitchen. "Fellas, will you find some table scraps for this stray?"

Ten minutes later, the kitten was enjoying a feast. Leftover scrambled eggs. A dollop of cold oatmeal. Half an English muffin. Even some creamed diced chicken.

The chef smiled. "Now, that's my kind of customer. He'll try anything,
eat everything, and never complain."

The headwaiter laughed. "You'll be hearing complaints if you don't get
back to work. We've got a full house this weekend. And there's a big contest
on Saturday. Bunch of fancy cats, I hear."

"Fancy cats," echoed the chef. Then he whispered to the kitten, "I'll take a
scrappy stray like you over a fancy cat any day."

The fancy cats began arriving later that afternoon. Cats from all over the country were coming to town for the Greater St. Louis Cat Club Show.

Royalty's Prince Sullen traveled from Jackson, Mississippi.

Northland Grey Cloud checked in after a long trip from Hannah, North Dakota.

Everyone noticed when Pearl Harbor Yank showed up from Bristol, Tennessee. He was very handsome—and very fussy.

The staff of the Hamilton Hotel was so busy welcoming the prestigious cats and their nervous companions that no one noticed the stray kitten sneak into the hotel lobby.

Not at first, anyway.

Hours later, Miss Marcella Duffy spotted the kitten in the kitchen.

"Who let you in?" she cried.

"Wasn't me," said the busboy.

"Not me," said the headwaiter.

"I didn't let him in," said the chef. "But I'm glad he's here.
Hey, kitty, kitty, you ever try smoked salmon?"

The kitten had never even heard of smoked salmon. He liked it immediately. He also liked the way it felt when the chef's daughter stroked his fur. Her name was Louise. She came to the hotel every day after school and on weekends to help her dad.

"Miss Duffy," said Louise, "should I put this cat outside?"

Marcella Duffy hesitated. "Yes. I mean, no. I mean, my goodness. It's still raining. Let him stay inside. I'm sure he won't disturb the guests."

The next day was Friday. Many of the fancy cats spent the day being groomed.

Other cats rested.

A few enjoyed a leisurely lunch in the hotel dining room.

The stray kitten couldn't resist trying to make a furry friend or two. Late in the afternoon, when no one was looking, he slipped into the dining room.

"Look at the filthy coat on that thing!" yelled a man.

"Smells like garbage," sneered a woman.

"I for one did not travel across the country to fraternize with a foul-smelling feline," growled another man. "Get it out of here!"

Miss Marcella Duffy swooped in, just in time. "I beg your humble pardon," she said as she scooped up the stray. As hostess, her job was to keep her guests happy and to apologize when anything made them unhappy.

Back in the kitchen, Marcella spoke gently to the kitten. "I'm so sorry you had to hear that. What they said about you is *not* true."

"Who needs 'em?" said the headwaiter. "Stick with us, kitty. You'll be safe back here."

"You ever try my dad's clam chowder?" asked Louise. "I think you'll like it."

The Cat Club Show began promptly on Saturday morning.
The aristocratic cats were divided into categories. When each class
was called, the entries were taken from the holding area to the
front of the hotel ballroom, where they were evaluated by judges.
Whiskers, claws, teeth, fur, even tails were all scrutinized.

After every category, a winner was announced. Champion
Carl's Pride won Best Manx. Bachelor's Bait won Best Novice.
And Pearl Harbor Yank? He was awarded three blue ribbons:
Best Champion, Best American-Bred Cat, and Best in Show.
At the end of the day, only two blue ribbons were left.

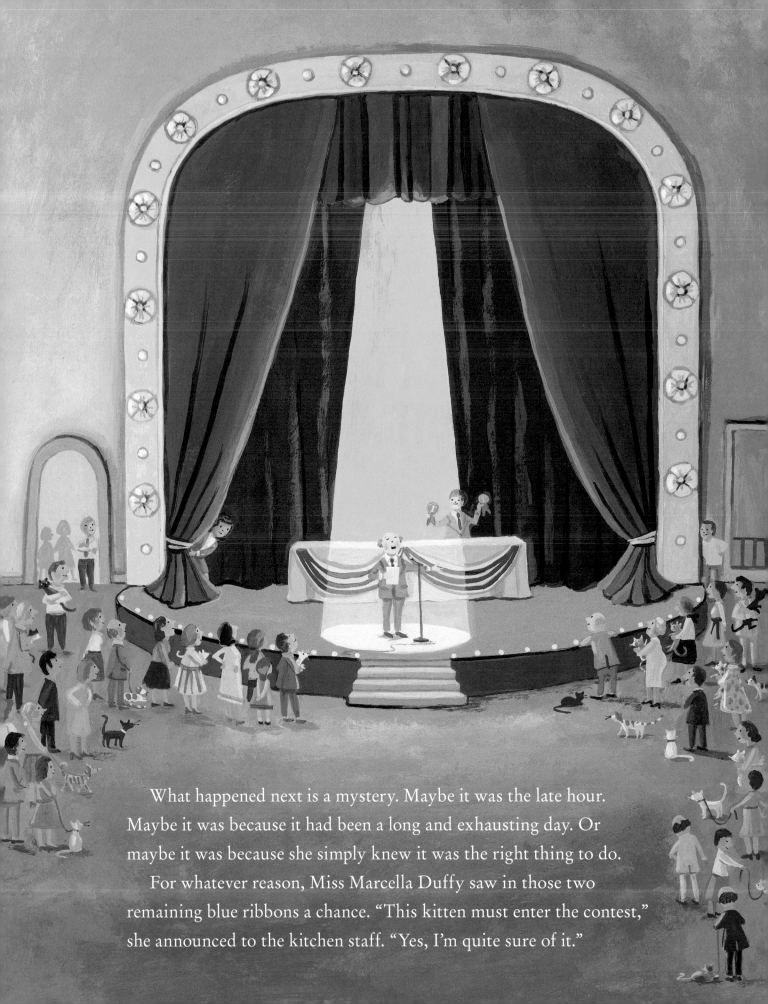

What happened next is a mystery. Maybe it was the late hour. Maybe it was because it had been a long and exhausting day. Or maybe it was because she simply knew it was the right thing to do. For whatever reason, Miss Marcella Duffy saw in those two remaining blue ribbons a chance. "This kitten must enter the contest," she announced to the kitchen staff. "Yes, I'm quite sure of it."

She used a smidgen of soap and a damp dishcloth to wash the cat.
Then, using her own hairbrush, she groomed him. "Here we go," she said.
"Wish us luck."

"That cat doesn't need luck," called the
headwaiter. "He's got personality!"

"Everybody loves an underdog!" cheered the chef.
"Especially when he's a cat."

Miss Duffy escorted the kitten to the judges' table.

"Where are the documents acknowledging this cat's pedigree?" asked the first judge.

"There are no documents," said Miss Duffy.

"How would you describe his ancestry?" the second judge inquired.

"I wouldn't," replied Miss Duffy.

"Is he well bred?" pressed the third judge.

"I haven't a clue," Miss Duffy replied.

"In that case," said the first judge, "we can't possibly consider this—"

Just then, Louise appeared in the ballroom. "Why can't you give him
a chance?" she asked. "He's the *sweetest* cat here."

Louise was right. There was something about the kitten. Even the
judges could see it once they gave him a closer look. This cat was scrappy.
He was curious. He was downright *charming.*

After conferring for several minutes, the judges awarded
the stray kitten not one but *two* blue ribbons.

The kitchen staff banged pots and pans to celebrate.
Louise grabbed a handful of silverware and jangled it loudly.

"Quiet, please!" scolded the first judge. "To make this official, I must know the name of this cat."

"His name?" asked Miss Duffy, biting her lip. She had no idea what the kitten's name was. But then her eyes locked on Louise and the shiny silverware she was holding.

"His name?" said Miss Duffy slowly. "Oh, that's easy. The cat's name is Mr. Silver."

Two days later, Mr. Silver made the front page of the *St. Louis Post-Dispatch*.

"No Pedigree, Just Charm," sang the headline of the *St. Louis Star-Times*.

"Alley Cat Wins Contest Honors," purred the *Cedar Rapids Gazette*.

The story was like catnip. No one could resist it. Nearly one hundred newspapers across the United States and Canada ran the story of Mr. Silver's victory, along with his photograph. Mr. Silver was famous!

But he was still a stray without a home. Mr. Silver couldn't stay at the Hamilton forever. It was a hotel for well-heeled people, not stray kittens. No one knew what to do.